RECITAL SUITE SERIES

ANSCHUTZ

Intermediate

THE CONNECTICUT RIVER

Betty Lea Martocchio

Mystic Schooner

Ivory Keys Rag

River Rhapsody

Memories of the Hockanum

Alfred

Mystic Schooner

Mystic Seaport, home to coastal schooners since the 17th century, was a leading shipbuilding center. Many Mystic schooners once sailed on the mighty Connecticut River. Mystic, a favorite vacation spot, has the country's leading maritime museum with the largest pictorial collection of boats and nautical photography in the world.

Betty Lea Martocchio

21
a tempo
f
25
rit.
a tempo
mf
29
mp
dim. e rit.
34
a tempo
f
39
mp
rit.
pp

Ivory Keys Rag

During the 19th century,* Comstock, Cheney & Company *in* Ivoryton *manufactured the vast majority of ivory piano keys, piano keyboards and piano actions in the country. By 1910, more than ninety percent of ivory imported from Africa had traveled up the Connecticut River to the nearby Essex Steamboat Dock, and was transported to the factory by horse and buggy. During this time, ragtime and honky-tonk piano playing and player pianos became the rage. The factory's recreational hall later became the famous Ivoryton Playhouse, a bustling theater venue that is still used for Broadway premieres and summer stock.

Betty Lea Martocchio

Lively (♩ = 132)

17
a tempo
mp
22
mf
rit.
f
a tempo
mf
27
f
32
36
mf
rit.
f
8va

River Rhapsody

Named "Quinnehtukgut" by the 17 Native American tribes that once inhabited most of New England, the Connecticut River, at 407 miles, is the longest river in the region. From Long Island Sound north to the growing cities of New England, the Connecticut River became a highway of commerce for Native Americans and European settlers. Its waterpower led to the rise of industrial cities along the river in the 19th century.

Betty Lea Martocchio

18
f
sfz
dim.
23
mp
molto rit.
27
a tempo
mf cresc.
32
rit.
sfz
a tempo
mp
37
rit.
pp

Memories of the Hockanum

In 1639, the Goodwin sawmill was built on the banks of the Hockanum River in Burnside village. Mills supplied General Washington's troops with everything from paper to gunpowder produced by the Pitkin Mill in Woodland to long underwear made by the Glastonbury Knitting Company. More than 1000 mills dotted the banks of the Connecticut River and its tributaries. The mills harnessed the rivers' energy, signaling the beginning of the Industrial Revolution in the United States.

Betty Lea Martocchio

17
a tempo
mp
21
25
mf
29
rit.

a tempo
33
p dolce
38
mf molto rit.
mp
42
8va
mf
p
46
a tempo
mp

50
ped. simile
54
mf
58
mp
rit.
62
p
pp

Alfred's

RECITAL SUITE SERIES was created for performing piano students. Each suite is a short collection of fresh-sounding solos carefully crafted to be played as a group in a recital. Musical challenges, appropriate for the level, provide interest and appeal. Aspiring pianists are challenged to reach higher degrees of excellence while playing music that is truly enjoyable for them and their audiences.

Dennis Alexander
The Carolinas (LI) 33895
The Great Northwest (LI) 23248
Kansas: The Sunflower State (LI) 29167
Vignettes of Hattiesburg (I) 37125

Melody Bober
The Dakotas (LI) 34420
The Great Lakes (LI) 28290
Impressions of Indiana (I) 37126
Postcards from Iowa (LI) 31814
Suite Alabama: A Jazz Sonatina (I) 31464

Dan Coates
Hollywood Dreams (LI) 27714

W. T. Skye Garcia
The Empire State (I) 24544

Tom Gerou

Joyce Grill
Minnesota Moments (I) 26138
Snapshots of Wisconsin (I) 27031

Marilynn Ham
Michigan Images (LI/EA) 22392

Randall Hartsell
Hawaiian Getaway (I) 23266

Andrew Higgins
Three Celtic Legends (LI/EA) 23249

Peter Jancewicz
Sketches of Canada (LI/EA) 22393

Bernadine Johnson
Land of Lincoln (LI) 29100
Nebraska: The Cornhusker State (I) 37127

Gayle Kowalchyk
The Lone Star State (I) 22427
New England Memories (I) 21322

Victor Labenske
Four Corners Suite (I) 22372
Show Me Missouri! (I) 27030
Sounds of Pennsylvania (I) 37128

Carol Matz
Our Nation's Capital (I) 31813

Betty Lea Martocchio
The Connecticut River (I) 37124

Martha Mier
Arkansas Suite (I) 20781
The Bluegrass State (LI) 31815
Florida Reflections (I) 22394
Louisiana Legacies (LI) 27028
Tennessee Treasures (LI) 34422

Catherine Rollin
The Grand Canyon (I) 34423
Mississippi Moods (I) 21397
Suite Georgia: A Sonatina (LI) 31913

Wynn-Anne Rossi
Along the Mississippi (LI) 34419

Mary K. Sallee
Oklahoma Heritage (LI) 24618

Mike Springer
Alaskan Adventures (I) 29099

Robert D. Vandall
Historic Virginia (I) 28984
Nevada Riches (LI) 27029
Ohio Skylines (LI) 24610
Scenes from the South (EI) 32090

The Connecticut River • Martocchio

Alfred

9780739077467
TP
APEX
37124 $4.50 in USA
0 38081 41241 2
ISBN 0-7390-7746-5